Comparing Bugs

Bug Parts

Charlotte Guillain

Heinemann Library
Chicago, Illinois

www.heinemannraintree.com
Visit our website to find out
more information about
Heinemann-Raintree books.

To order:

☎ Phone 888-454-2279

🖳 Visit www.heinemannraintree.com
to browse our catalog and order online.

Edited by Rebecca Rissman and Catherine Veitch
Designed by Joanna Hinton-Malivoire
Picture research by Elizabeth Alexander
Production by Duncan Gilbert and Victoria Fitzgerald
Originated by Heinemann Library
Printed and bound in China by South China Printing
Company Ltd

14 13 12 11 10
10 9 8 7 6 5 4 3 2 1

Library of Congress Cataloging-in-Publication Data
Bug parts / Charlotte Guillain. -- 1st ed.
p. cm. -- (Comparing bugs)
ISBN 978-1-4329-3565-8 (hc) -- ISBN 978-1-4329-3574-0 (pb)
QL467.2.G8566 2010
595.7--dc22
                        2009025543

Acknowledgments
The author and publishers are grateful to the following for permission
to reproduce copyright material: Alamy pp. **15** (© Arco Images GmbH),
19 (© blickwinkel); Ardea.com p. **21** (© M. Watson); FLPA p. **12** (© Thomas
Marent/Minden Pictures); iStockphoto pp. **13** (© Viorika Prikhodko), **22
bottom right**, **23 bottom** (© Ben Twist); Photolibrary pp. **4** (Juniors
Bildarchiv), **18** (Michael Weber/imagebroker.net), **23 top** (Michael Weber/
imagebroker.net); Shutterstock pp. **5** (© Ervin Monn), **8** (© photobar), **9** (©
EuToch), **7** (© yxm2008), **6** (© Orlov Mihail Anatolevich), **10** (© Yellowj),
11 (© Ed Phillips), **16** (© Miles Boyer), **17** (© Miles Boyer), **14** (© Kirsanov),
20 (© David Dohnal), **22 left** (© Jens Stolt), **22 top right** (© Subbotina
Anna), **23 middle bottom** (©Yellowj).

Cover photograph of ants and aphids on a stem reproduced with
permission of Photolibrary (Creativ Studio Heinemann/Westend61). Back
cover photograph of a spider on an iris flower reproduced with permission
of Shutterstock (© Ed Phillips).

The publishers would like to thank Nancy Harris and Kate Wilson for their
assistance in the preparation of this book.

Every effort has been made to contact copyright holders of any material
reproduced in this book. Any omissions will be rectified in subsequent
printings if notice is given to the publisher.

Contents

Meet the Bugs

There are many different types
of bugs.

head

legs

Bugs have different body parts.

Bodies

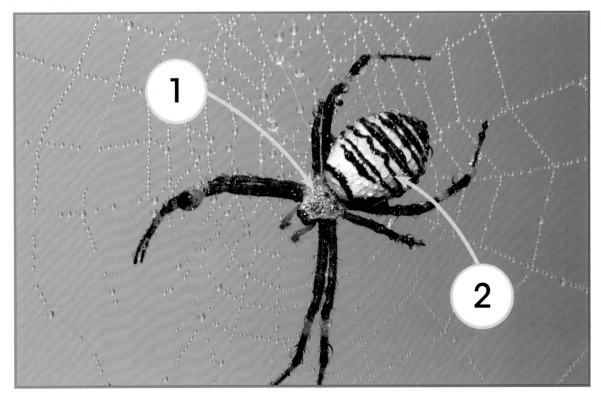

Spiders have two body parts.

Insects have three body parts.

Bugs do not have backbones.

shell

Some bugs have shells.

Legs

legs

Insects have six legs.

Spiders have eight legs.

legs

Millipedes have many legs.

Worms have no legs.

Wings

wings

Some bugs have wings.

Bugs use their wings to fly.

Some bugs use their wings to scare birds away.

Some bugs use their wings to hide.

Antennae

antennae

Some bugs have antennae.

antennae

Bugs use antennae to feel, taste, and smell.

Stings and Bites

stinger

Some bugs can sting.

claws

Some bugs can bite.
Centipedes bite with claws.

How Big?

ladybug

moth

millipede

Look at how big some of the bugs in this book can be.

Picture Glossary

antenna long, thin feeler on the head of an insect

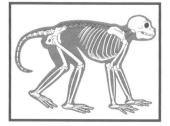
backbone row of bones down the middle of the back

insect very small creature with six legs

shell hard body covering

Index

Notes to Parents and Teachers

Before reading

Make a list of bugs with the children. Try to include insects, arachnids (e.g. spiders), crustaceans (e.g. wood lice), myriapods (e.g. centipedes and millipedes,) and earthworms. Then ask them what body parts they think each bug has. Do they know how many legs each bug on the list has? Do they know which bugs have wings? What else do they know about bug bodies? Give the children a brief description of a backbone, what it is, and which animals have one.

After reading

• Between spring and late summer you could go on a bug hunt. Put the children into groups and give each group a plastic pot, a paintbrush, and a magnifying glass. Go out into the school grounds and look under stones and leaves for bugs. Show the children how they can gently pick up bugs using the paintbrush bristles, put them into the plastic pot, then look at them under a magnifying glass. Emphasize how important it is to treat living creatures carefully and to put them back where they were found. Ask the children to try to identify the bugs they find and look at their body parts. Share their findings at the end of the hunt.

• Make a table to record the children's findings. Put the name of each bug at the top of each column and label each row with a different body part, e.g. legs, wings, antennae. For each bug put a tick or cross to show which body parts it has and record the number of parts if applicable.

• Remind the children that insects have six legs. Which of the bugs on their table are insects and which are not?